Keeper's Tail

Keeper's Tail

How a Golden Retriever, Born Blind, Finds Her Way Through

Life and Into Your Heart!

By JAMIE PEDERSON

Keeper's Tail

Copyright © 2019 by Jamie Pederson

All rights reserved.

ISBN 978-1-7336432-1-4

Jamie Pederson

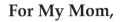

For My Mom,

For loving me and always being there. For giving me the strength to step outside my comfort zone and try new things. And for getting me through the hard stuff.

I love you!

Jamie

For Keeper, Joey, Robbi and all my Fur Covered Companions,

For accepting me for exactly who I am and for being extraordinarily cute and cuddly. For making my life infinitely better and loving me unconditionally.

Thank you for doing life with me!

For my grandchildren Amaya, Avrey, Abbey, Ajay, Morgan, Landon, Felicity, Eloise, and any future grandchildren,

If you inherit anything from me, I hope it is the ability to Love and Fully Appreciate the Unconditional Love of an animal.

~ Acknowledgments

Turning an idea into a book is hard. The experience is difficult and leaves you feeling vulnerable. I especially want to thank the individuals who supported me through the process.

Martina Tangen ~ Thank you for your edits and suggestions and for putting up with my tantrums and self-doubt! Most of all, thank you for your love, patience, encouragement, and reassurance through the process! I could have done it without you, but it wouldn't have been nearly as much fun.

Leslie Rausch-Sligh ~ Thank you for helping me through the GRLS donation approval process and for your love and support.

Author Pam Maxey (and Joey) ~ Thank you for your advice and guidance.

My Husband Brad, My Mom & Dad, Sue Dunlap, Danette Mapula and other Family and Friends ~ Without your love, support and patience this book would not exist.

Contents

~ Introduction ~

*H*i there, my name is Keeper Malachi, but you can call me Keeper. Names are the sounds people use to get my attention. I cannot make name sounds like people do, but I know what my name sounds like and that it means a people is talking to me. My Mom uses many names for me, some I like (because Mom is using her happy voice), like Silly Girl, Fluffy Butt, Sweetheart, Sister, and Sweet Pea. These are love names, or nicknames.

There are also names I don't like (because Mom is using her angry or annoyed voice), like No-No-No, Stop, Bad, Down, or when she puts my two names together and says very loud **KEEPER MALACHI!** These names help me know Mom does not like what I am doing, and I need to stop.

I have one name that confuses me, Blind! Mom uses this name to people we haven't smelled before. When Mom tells people I am Keeper and I am blind, they make sad people noises and want to give me love-touches. I like the touches, but the sadness confuses me.

Mom wants to share my story with you because she loves me big, and because I am also named Special and Inspiring. She will call my story "Keeper's Tail." I don't know what my tail has to do with it, but Mom told me it's a metaphor, because like my tail the story will follow me. Silly Mom! Anyway, it is so nice of you to read my story and I hope you like it.

Jamie Pederson

~ Forever Home ~

I don't remember much before I smelled Mom the first time. I remember being around other little ones like me, and a bigger one who took care of and fed us. Mom said the big one is the Mother and the little ones are Siblings.

The first time I smelled my Mom was exciting and scary! It was the early part of awake time called morning, when Mom and Friend-Martina came to hold and love me. People like to give me touches and loves because I am extremely cute and adorable. Mom held me close while she said words to the people where I lived, and then she took me away in a big noisy thing called a car-truck. I was still very tiny and not very tough and I did not like the car-truck. I like car-truck rides now because they take me to lots of fun places.

Martina was very nice; she wrapped me in a blanket and held me in her lap. I was scared and shaking and Martina helped me by saying words in a quiet voice and touching me a lot. The Siblings and Mother didn't go with us. I whined for most of the ride because I didn't want to go away from them; they were all I knew!

For most of the long ride Mom talked too, she said she is my new Mama and she will love and protect me forever. Mom told me I have a perfect little under bite and a perfectly crooked nose, and I couldn't be cuter or more precious. I don't know what these words mean, but she still tells me this a lot. Mom also told me my name is Keeper Malachi; but like I said, I have lots of names. I guess when you get a new home and a new Mom; you get a new name too.

When we got out of the car-truck, we were not at the home with Mother and Siblings any more. Mom said this is my new and forever home. She said I was only five and a half weeks old and I weighed less than five pounds. I don't know what these words mean either, but they seemed to make my Mom very sad.

The first day at my new-and-forever home, was the last time I smelled the Siblings and Mother. I was scared and sad for a while. I was very nervous and afraid about learning to find my way around. I knew life in my new home would be hard without the help of the Siblings and Mother. I already missed the familiar smells, the comfort of snuggles and loves, and the play times with them. Things were very different here; I hoped it would be good for me to be Keeper Malachi.

From that first day, I have been with my new-forever-family, in my new-forever home; but it is a great thing! One of the first things I noticed was the strong and wonderful smell of two others like me. I met Brother Joey and Sister RobbiLynn and learned they also lived in my new home. They have lots of other names too, and some of them are the same as mine (which is confusing).

Brother Joey reminds me of the smell of the Mother and Siblings, so I think he came from the same first home place I did. It was nice to have something familiar to my nose. Joey seemed to think I smelled good too, and he touched me a lot with his nose.

~ First Day ~

*T*he first day with Mom was hard. I was confused and not sure what was going on. Mom and Martina tried to help me with love-touches and snuggles. The day was busy with lots of new smells, noises, and touches for me. We sat on the grass in the front yard. Martina smelled good, like she has loved and touched others like me. I could tell right away that Martina knows how wonderful, cute and adorable I am, and I was already her favorite!

The grass felt nice to my puppy feet, and it smelled wonderful. While I was bumping around, Mom said "potty-potty" several times. I didn't know these words yet, but I would figure them out.

My cute little puppy feet are very smart and they help me know stuff by how it feels. While I was walking around, I felt something that didn't feel nice, so I tried to pull it out of the grass with my puppy teeth. Mom made a happy people noise called laughing, and she said, "Keeper, those are weeds and you can pull them all out." I enjoyed hearing Mom make the laughing noise!

While I smelled around, Mom kept saying "Careful Keeper," at first, I didn't pay much attention. Before long I noticed that when Mom said "Careful Keeper" I hit my nose on something. I decided "Carefuls" hurt! Now when Mom says "Careful" I pay attention. I learned that how close the "careful" is, changes with the way Mom says it. If Mom says careful like any other word, the "careful" is not close, but a loud and fast "Careful," is much closer. Careful is the first word I learned to listen for.

I explored the grass in the front yard, smelling with my nose and feeling with my smart-puppy-feet. My ears heard RobbiLynn and Joey in the nice grass too. Before long they came close, to smell me and poked their noses at me. I could tell they thought I was cute and adorable, and they wanted to know what I was doing.

I'm pretty smart and figured out Joey and RobbiLynn didn't know what to do with the grass either. I think they were hoping I would show them. Soon I felt the need, so I squatted to wet. Mom got excited and said "Good-Girl, good potty" over and over, then she picked me up and snuggled me a lot. Martina said I was Good-Girl too. I decided I like the Good-Girl name. I hope they name this at me a lot! After I wet the grass, Robbi and Joey wet the grass too, when Mom said the Good name at them, I knew I was a big help.

After some time on the nice grass, we went inside the home for the first time. Inside the home smelled strong of Mom, Robbi, and Joey. There was a new smell too, I would get to meet him later and learn his name is Dad. It didn't take long to understand that Mom, Dad, RobbiLynn and Joey are my new-and-forever family!

My new-and-forever home soon became just "home," and my new-and-forever family, just "family!" My life in this home with this family would be very different from what I was used to. When my family is inside the home, I am inside with them, and when they are outside, I am outside too. Being inside a home was new because I had never been in a home part before. I like it a lot!

When I am inside, there is no cold or hot pushing on me! There is always food and water, a cozy place to nap, and toys. I've never had toys before. I like toys! In this home, there is a big box of toys for me to choose from anytime I want.

On the first day, I had lots of short sleeps called naps. Between my naps, people came to smell me; this is called meeting or visits. I got to smell Sister- Jeannie; Jeannie liked it when I licked on her face and said she liked my puppy breath.

After more naps I got to smell Friend-Danette; Danette was nice too. She smelled like a new puppy friend I would get to meet later.

After a long time and a lot of naps, I finally got to smell Dad. He said the hello words at my ears, but I could hear Joey and Robbi were excited and jumping all over him. Dad couldn't get away to smell me and get to know how cute and adorable I am, so that would have to wait until later.

I smelled many people between naps, and I got lots of love-touches. I noticed that everyone has lots of different names just like me. The Brother and Sister who live in the forever-home are called by their Joey and Robbi names. But they have lots of the same names I do, like Fluffy Butt, Silly and Sweetheart. The big people who live in the forever-home are Mom and Dad, but people use other names, like Jamie and Brad.

That day I began to understand I was home now, and this is my family. I learned they will always love and protect me, and I will never have to leave. This is how I learned what Family is!

Jamie Pederson

~ Mom & Dad ~

*I*t didn't take long for me to know that Mom's job is to love me and keep me safe. When I am feeling anxious or scared, I find Mom, and she makes everything ok. Mom and Dad are very different. I figured out that Dad's job is playing, and he is good at it! Sometimes Mom plays with me and sometimes Dad loves on me, but I usually go to Dad if I want to play and Mom if I want love.

Mom talks a lot more than Dad does. Mom sends words right to my ears saying "Keeper" to get my attention. I love when Mom talks, it helps me know that she loves me and I am not alone.

Dad gives me people food; I like people food. When Mom knows Dad gave me people food, she says his name loud, "BRAD," and tells him to stop. Then Mom tells Dad he will love me to death. I don't understand these words except the Love word, and it's okay for Dad to love me with food and Mom to love me with words and touches!

One of my most favorite places in the whole world is in Mom or Dads lap. I like to be in their lap while I chew on a toy so they can touch and love me. I don't like it when Joey and Robbi get there first, so I jump on top of them until they move and I get the lap all to myself. Mom calls me Brat when I do this and tells me Robbi and Joey need Mom and Dad time too.

Now I am bigger and I can't put all myself into a lap anymore, so I put the part I want touched. Sometimes Joey and Robbi don't let me be a Brat because they need their Mom and Dad time! When this happens, Mom says I have to wait my turn. I don't like this wait stuff!

Mom tries to keep me safe, but sometimes she is sorry and I get hurt. When I get hurt, Mom feels terrible, like she wasn't smart and didn't do her job; she gives me lots of love words and touches. I wish I could make the people's word noises to tell Mom how much I love her, and to let her know she is doing good for me. I try to tell Mom things by following her around or lying on her feet.

Sometimes I use noises like whining. I don't think Mom understands because she says "What," "Are you OK," "Are you hurt," and "What do you need." I don't think people understand dog noises at all!

I love everyone; I like to run and play and smell everyone! But when it's time for the long sleep called night, I need to be at home with my family. That's the way it is and I don't want it to change. I know Robbi and Joey feel the same way. Sometimes we have time at home without Mom and Dad called "you-can't-go".

We don't like you-can't-go, and we never know when it will happen. We whine and get very sad and try to tell them we need to go too. There are also times Mom takes one of us and the others have you-can't-go. If Mom takes me to smell the doctor ladies or we walk without Robbi and Joey, this is called Keeper time.

I like Keeper time with Mom, and it makes me feel special to be the one that gets to go. I don't like it at all if Mom takes Robbi time or Joey time! Robbi and Joey don't like Keeper time either. Even though I like Keeper time, I sometimes wish Robbi and Joey could go too because I miss them. They help me with the carefuls when Mom forgets.

There are also times called vacation and weekend. These are days we get to be with Mom and Dad almost the whole time. They are the same except vacation is more days and nights than a weekend. And we have more weekends than vacations. I love vacation and weekend times the best because Mom and Dad are home with no go-to-work. For vacation and weekend times sometimes, other people come to visit at our home, or we go visit their homes.

Jamie Pederson

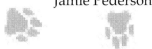

~ Robbi and Joey ~

I am so happy RobbiLynn and Joey are my family; they help me know how to do things and what I am not supposed to do. Mom said Joey is two years old, and Robbi is seven years old. Mom also told me Joey has the same mother as me; I think this is why he smells like her and the siblings we left behind.

Joey has another name, "Hero." Joey is "Hero" because he is part of the [1]Golden Retriever Lifetime Study (GRLS). The GRLS is for helping others like us, named Golden Retriever, not get sick. Mom says she is very proud of Joey.

When I first met RobbiLynn, she wasn't very nice, I think it's because RobbiLynn is older and she is not

---

[1] Golden Retriever Lifetime Study by the Morris Animal Foundation, for more information visit https://www.morrisanimalfoundation.org/golden-retriever-lifetime-study

patient. I didn't mind that Robbi wasn't friendly with me, because Joey loves me a lot and looks out for me all the time. I played with Joey and tried not to annoy RobbiLynn. Sometimes it was hard for me to have RobbiLynn close and not love and play with her. I hoped she would figure out how cute and adorable I am soon.

Joey loves to play rough with me, but he is careful and helps me a lot too! When I play rough with Joey, Robbi barks at us and tells us how to play. This is annoying; I already know how to play! I wish Robbi would tell me things I don't know, like how not to bump into the carefuls. I don't need to be told how to play.

Sometimes I play hide with Joey, but he is much better than I am. I try to hold very still so Joey can't hear me with his ears. Joey must have good ears to hear me breathe, or a good nose to smell me because he always finds me fast. I can find Joey by holding still so I can hear him breathe or smell him close, but I'm not as good as Joey is. Even when Joey is far away, he has no trouble finding me. I hope I get that good someday too. For now, I try to be still and quiet so Joey has a hard time finding me. Mom said Joey is cheating because he uses something called seeing; I hope I learn seeing soon, so I can cheat too!

When Mom and Dad are gone from the home during the day, we wait for them to come back. Sometimes Robbi gets toys to carry around and tease me. If I try to take the toys away, Robbi is too quick and I can't get them! I'm very sneaky, and most of the time I pretend I don't care until Robbi drops the toy, and then I grab it quick and run away.

Joey only gets toys from the box if he wants me to play with him. Joey brings the toy and pushes it on my face until I try to take it, then runs away and I get to chase him. I like playing and never say no. But we don't play very much while Mom and Dad are not at home because we are sad and waiting.

When Mom and Dad come home, we meet them at the door-hole and bring toys; we are happy and excited. Mom names me "Down," and "Calm," and we do what she calls wiggle-butt, because we can't help ourselves. They give us "come-home-cookies" and lots of love-touches and nice words. Then, because we can't wait anymore, Mom lets us to the outside backyard, to wet the grass called "potty-potty" and run around.

Sometimes Mom talks about Josie Lou, when she does, she gets sad. I can tell when Mom is sad because there is salty water on her face and she needs me to love and cuddle her. I am always happy to love and cuddle on Mom, but I don't like when she is sad. Mom gets sad about other names too, like Maxine, Pooh and Samantha. I wonder who these names are and why they are not here if Mom loves them so much. Mom said I remind her of Josie Lou, and we would have been great friends and loved each other.

There are smells of others like me in the home, but they are not very strong smells. I think they have been gone for a long time. I wonder if Josie Lou is one of those smells. Maybe Mom is sad because the smells don't live here anymore. I don't know why anyone would leave; I already love it here and I hope I never have to go away from my new mom and forever home.

I love my Robbi and Joey, but I wish they would run and play more. One day I heard Mom tell Dad "Keeper is afraid to run because she can't see." I'm pretty smart, but I don't understand these words yet, so I will keep listening and try to figure them out.

~ Go-to-work ~

*H*ome is good. At home there is always Joey and Robbi, and except for "go-to-work" and "you-can't-go" times, there is always Mom and Dad. When I was very little, for go-to-work times I had to stay in the go-to-work kennel. The kennel is a small area away from Robbi and Joey, where I was all by myself. I didn't like the kennel because I was alone! Since the kennel felt safe, like no one would step on me and there were no carefuls to find with my nose, I tried to sleep.

When Mom put me in the kennel, I whined and barked to let her know I didn't like it, but she didn't listen! If I whine and bark, Joey listens, and he gets worried. I whined every time, so Joey would come and lay next to the kennel where I could smell and touch him. Joey is the best big brother, and he helps me not feel so afraid and alone. I was happy to learn the kennel was only until Mom came home each day.

For the first days at my new home, Mom said we were on vacation. This vacation was 10 days and nights. For all 10 days I got to be with my family, we stayed at our home and had lots of outside playing on the grass time. I learned that vacation times are special family time and they don't happen often. Family time means we are all together, whether we are in the home or we go places in the car-truck. Going in the car-truck is my favorite!

Learning is hard, but lots of good comes from it. I learned when I make the wet called "potty-potty," I am supposed to do it outside the home. I also figured out they call poop potty-potty too, and all potty-potty goes outside the home. It took a while and a lot of reminders, but Mom, Robbi, and Joey taught me to always do potty-potty in the grass, every time! I was happy when I got bigger and understood that if I do potty-potty on the grass outside, I don't have to be in the go-to-work kennel anymore! Going outside to do potty-potty also helped me not have the No-No-No name I don't like. I am one smart puppy!

Now that I am good at doing all potty-potty outside, the go-to-work kennel is gone. I don't know what happened to it, but I am sure happy it's gone. With no more kennel I get to be with Robbi and Joey when Mom and Dad are not at home. I still think it's best to sleep though. If Mom and Dad are not at home for a long time, I take breaks from sleeping to play with Joey and Robbi. When they come home, we play and walk and I don't want to miss anything fun because I am too tired. Sleeping while they are gone is good.

When Mom comes home, she is so excited to see me, almost like she didn't expect me to still be here! I know Mom worries about me a lot because she says, "How are you doing Keeper." This means Mom needs me, and she is scared I will go away. I try to tell her I'm not going anywhere because I know she needs me, and I need her too! Mom doesn't understand my puppy noises like I understand her peoples' words.

When Mom and Dad come home, they have new smells and sometimes smells we already know. We like to snuff all over them called sniffing. It's fun to try to figure out where they have been and who they visited while they were gone. They are never gone for the long sleep times; it's nice to know they will always be home soon. If they are gone for a long time, I get worried they won't make it home for the long sleep. I worry a lot; Mom tells me not to worry, but that doesn't work!

One day they were getting ready for go-to-work and Mom said, "Keeper, do you want to go?" Is she crazy, I want to go, I always want to go! Mom put a coat on me and she said, "This is to let everyone know you are working," then we went for a ride in the car-truck. For this ride, she let me be in the part called seat so I could put my head in her lap. Joey and Robbi didn't get to go.

When the ride was over, we went through the door-hole of a home that smelled like lots of people. The smell was the same as Mom when she comes home from go-to-work, so I knew we were there. I didn't smell Dad at this go-to-work place. But he smells different when he comes home so he must have a different go-to-work home.

I got to smell a lot of nice people who said things like "Hello," "Aren't you cute," and "What a sweetheart." After the words, smells, and touches, we went to a place that smelled a lot like Mom. For the rest of go-to-work time Mom sat in a chair and I put my head on her feet like at home. People came to say hello and give me love. That is all we did, so I don't know why they want to leave us every day for go-to-work!

A lot of days later, we had "Keeper's" go-to-work, and it was much better. Keeper's go-to-work was at a different work home. There was a new smell I have never smelled before, and there were a lot of little people kids. One of the kids had a Happy Birthday. I think that is why we went!

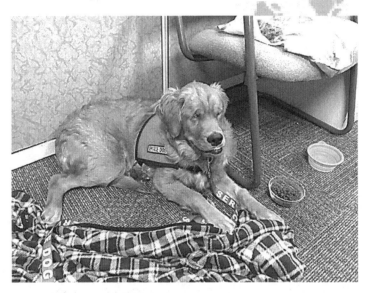

There were a lot of words all at one time. I get very anxious if there is a lot of word noise because I can't catch all the words with my ears. Mom stayed close and touched me a lot saying, "It's okay, you're okay, be calm, you're a Good-Girl" in quiet words close to my ear.

The kids bumped into me a lot and everyone was calling me the Blind name. I stayed close to Mom and played the listen game. I heard the kids called the Blind name too. I have never heard anyone else called

Blind before, not even Robbi and Joey! Mom also called Keeper's go-to-work "School for the Blind."

At first, I didn't think I would like it here because it was loud and noisy, and I didn't know where the carefuls were. I stayed close to Mom with my head on her feet. Everyone wanted to smell and love-touch me a lot, but these touches were different. When people give me love-touches they usually touch the top of my head and down my back, or on my tummy (which I love). These kids were touching all over my head and face like when Mom checks to feel if I am Ok-alright.

At this go-to-work there were other Fur-Kids too, but they didn't want to play or even smell me. They stayed close with their kids and they were very rude and ignored me. Mom said, "These dogs are working; this is what you are learning." I'm not sure I want to learn to be rude, but I like the go-to-work time, so I will try it.

We went back to Keeper's go-to-work a few days later; this time I wasn't as scared because I knew the smells and noises. There were new people to smell, and I walked around more, so that was good. Mom helped me know I am supposed to sit, be calm, and let the kids smell and love-touch me. They still touched me like Mom does to check for hurt. I guess they love a little different than other people, but it's OK, I like all kinds of loves!

~ Words ~

*L*ike I said earlier, Mom talks a lot! She told me, "Keeper, I talk to you because you can't see and words will help you see with your ears." I remember Mom saying Joey uses the seeing trick to cheat, and now she is trying to teach me to cheat too. When Mom says the same word a lot of times, it helps me learn. Some words I learn because they tell me what things are. When Mom touches me and says, "These are Keepers ears," "This is Keepers nose," and "This is Keepers tail." I learn the word name.

There are also words I don't get to feel with a touch, words like, I love you Keeper, dinner is ready, and let's go for a walk. These "only hear" words make me feel good inside my tummy, like the laughing noise!

There are words to help me, like the "careful" word to help me not run into things. And words to explain how I feel, like I get "hurt" if no one tells me when there is a careful in my way. Words can tell me what to do, like come, sit and stay. I'm learning new words every day.

When I first came to my new home and was still tiny, Mom carried me a lot. One day Mom said, "Keeper, you need to learn the house," and she stopped carrying me. After that I kept bumping into stuff inside the home. Mom was already using the careful word before I bumped into stuff, and I knew careful means I will hit something.

Mom started using the same careful word inside the home. I learned where all the carefuls are, and as long as they don't move, I can avoid them… most of the time! Learning where the carefuls are inside the home helps me feel safe. Robbi and Joey help me find my way too. Mom told me I'm getting good at seeing with my ears. This means I hear noises that tell me where stuff is, so I don't bump into carefuls and get hurt as much.

I don't understand how Joey and Robbi know where the carefuls are; they seem to know without being told! There must be a trick to knowing because I don't hear others bumping into them. Maybe this is the seeing trick Mom calls cheating, and I can learn as I grow bigger; I have a lot to learn.

Sometimes Mom puts a lot of words together like, "Wait, I am opening-the-door." At first, I didn't understand these words. But I learned if I don't "wait" (which is like the stay word), I run into the "door." If I wait until Mom says "Okay," or until I hear the opening-the-door noise, I can go without hitting my head. I learned to wait!

I learned that walk is a very good word. "Go" is good as long as go isn't with other words like "I have to go-to-work" or "you-can't-go this time." These words together mean only Mom and Dad get to go! Learning is hard, but Mom tells me I am one smart puppy and I will do fine.

I am not able to make people's word noises, so I try to use the noises I can make, like barking and whining. Sometimes when I bark or whine, I get what I want; like food, a touch, or playtime.

Sometimes I try to help Mom and Dad know what I want by using my puppy feet to touch them. I am very careful not to touch too hard because I don't want anyone to get hurt. When I touch Mom with my foot, she makes the laughing sound and calls me Cute. I think Mom likes touches as much as I do!

Another way I can help others understand is by bringing them something. I bring a bowl if I want food, a toy to say I want to play, or pillow for sleep and snuggles.

I try to listen to Mom so I know what she wants. But I think Mom is confused about words too. Sometimes she uses the same word for different things! Like when Mom calls me **No-No-No**, this means stop whatever I am doing. But if I whine or bark and Mom says, "I don't **know** what you want." The **Know** word sounds the same as the telling me to stop **No-No-No**.

If Mom says "I am going to **close** the door" I know this means I will hit the door if I try to go outside. But if Mom says, "I'm going to change my **clothes** so we can walk!" This confuses me! If we are going to walk does "change my clothes" mean un-closing the door?

47

Word talk can be very confusing; even Mom doesn't get it sometimes.

When Mom moves the carefuls around inside the home, she tells me so I don't find them with my head and get hurt. Dad isn't as good about telling me when he moves carefuls, or leaves them in my way.

If Dad doesn't tell me he moved carefuls, Mom says words at him loud; "Keeper cannot see, you need to be more careful!" I don't like loud words! I don't understand how Mom knows Dad left carefuls? Maybe Dad found carefuls with is nose, so Mom is using loud words to tell him the same way she tells me. But it doesn't sound like she checks Dad's face and nose for hurt to see if he is Ok-alright.

~ Walks ~

Walk is one of my favorite words: Soon after I got to my new home, we went outside for walks. This walk stuff was hard for me at first because I had to learn how walks work. For walks Mom puts something around my neck called "Collar," the collar connects to something called "Leash." At first, I didn't like the way the collar wrapped around my neck, but I got used to it pretty quickly and it was OK. The leash

49

is Terrible! The lease won't let me run and play, and if I try while the leash is on, Mom says in her frustrated or annoyed voice "No-Pull."

I try hard to No-Pull (which I soon understood means stop trying to get away from the leash), but it is very hard because I get excited about being outside, and I want to run and play. I have gotten better; now if I feel the leash get tight, I walk a big circle all the way around Mom. She still says No-Pull sometimes. Like when I find new smells, or I hear others around and I want to get love-touches or run and play.

As I have gotten bigger, Mom lets me be off the leash sometimes. I am off the leash even more now that I am a big girl and I do what Mom calls "minding" or "behaven"... well, most of the time. If I am not "minding" or "behaven" Mom says, "Keeper, do you want your pants in trouble?" This means Mom will have angry or annoyed words, and I have to be attached to the leash again.

There are lots of times Mom keeps the leash on me, even when I'm good. This is because we go new places and she doesn't know where all the carefuls are. I don't like the leash, but I am learning not to try to get away from it. If I am good at staying close to

Mom, I get to be Good-Girl; I like the Good-Girl name. If I try to get away from the leash fast, I hear Mom make noises that tell me she is hurt. When this happens, she says "No-Pull" in her loud voice. I love Mom and I don't want her to have hurt.

Mom loves me very big; when I get hurt, it makes her worried and scared for me. When I find carefuls on the trail, she touches me all over. If I don't have hurt, I am Ok-alright! Sometimes when I am off the leash, Mom forgets to tell me about carefuls and I find them with my head or nose. If I am going fast and find a careful, it causes loud HURT. When this happens, Mom comes quickly to check my face and nose and ask if I am "Ok-alright." Then Mom gives me extra love-touches and says she is sorry. Sorry means Mom was being careless and let me run into carefuls. I wish Mom would stop being sorry!

Because Mom doesn't like calling me No-Pull, she tried to fix it. She tried new things called harness and gentle-lead instead of the collar. I do not like the harness because it wraps all over me and it doesn't feel good when I try to get away. I hate the gentle-lead! When she put the gentle-lead on me, I tried to get it off with my smart-puppy-feet! When it wouldn't come off, I refused to move! The gentle-lead goes across my nose and doesn't feel good at all, but Mom only tried it a few times, so that's good.

If I hear noises that mean Mom is getting the harness, I hide away so she can't put it on me. Mom always finds me though, and she puts the harness on. After a while, I learned the harness means we get to walk the trail. Now I let Mom put it on even though I don't like it. I still pout for a few minutes to let her know I'm unhappy, but then we get to go and I forget I'm mad. The harness doesn't feel good if I try to get away, and that reminds me to be a Good-Girl so Mom doesn't have to say No-Pull.

When we are on the trail, I smell many people and their Fur-Kids. Sometimes these are people I have smelled before. If I have smelled them before, Mom might let me go close so they can say hello and give love-touches. Sometimes we smell "one-time" people on the trail. For one-time people, Mom says, "Keeper, No visit-No-bark." No-visit-No-bark means I don't get to say hello or get love-touches. When I am good with No-visit-No-bark, I get to be Good-Girl! Mom also calls the Good name to Robbi and Joey, but I still like it, even if it's not for me.

As I have gotten better with behaven, I get to be off the leash more. I learned there are a lot of carefuls outside the home. I can use my smart-puppy-feet to help me miss most of the carefuls by staying on the trail. I know when I am on the trail because it feels different when I step off. If my smart-puppy-feet tell me I have stepped off the trail I change direction until my feet feel the trail again. This way I miss most of the carefuls called trees.

If we have walked a trail before and I'm comfortable with it, Mom will let me be in front and I can go fast. I can also go fast when I follow Joey and Robbi because they help me know where the carefuls are. But if I try to follow them when they chase noises I can't keep up and I hit the carefuls and get hurt. I am one smart puppy, so I don't chase noises with Robbi and Joey!

Some trails are hard because the tree-carefuls are right on the edge. If the tree-carefuls are too close to the trail, I don't get to feel the off-the-trail warning with my smart feet. If Mom doesn't warn me with the careful word, I hit them. My mom is smart about carefuls, most of the time she lets me know there is a careful before I find it with my head or nose. Sometimes Mom waits until I am close and has to say CAREFUL fast and loud so I stop.

Carefuls have lots of names too; they can be a Car, Tree, People, Fence, Chair, and many other names. Mom always calls them "Careful" for me; this way I know she is telling me there is something in my way. When I get excited, I sometimes forget to listen for the careful word. If I don't listen, I can get loud hurt. Mom uses other words to help me; like Step, this way and Stop. But she uses the careful word the most!

We go on walks every day and they have different walk names. There are "morning walks," "windy walks," "sunset walks," frosty walks, birthday walks, to name a few. I think Mom is being silly; like when she calls me Fluffy Butt or Ornery. Where does she get this stuff!

When we have walks and playing, it's easy for me to be distracted, I do silly things like run into Mom and Dad. One day I ran into Mom very hard, she sat on the trail and made the noises that let me know it hurt her. Even though it was Mom's hurt, she checked me for Ok-alright. This time I was the one being sorry!

For a long time after I ran into Mom, her leg was wrapped in something that felt hard to my head when I bumped it. While she was wearing this very hard leg-sleeve, she walked with sticks called crutches. With the leg-sleeve called Cast, and crutches-sticks, Mom didn't go on the walks with us, so Dad took us for walks alone.

Mom had the crutches-sticks with her wherever she went for a lot of days. I don't know why she wanted to have them since they were no fun at all. I was very worried because I didn't want Mom to have crutches-sticks forever. They were hard for me to get around and I bumped them a lot.

While Mom was using the crutches-sticks, she would sit and scoot up and down the stair-steps. I loved Mom sitting on the stair-steps and we had too much fun! She was down at my level and I would get on her lap and lick her face. Mom told me to stop, but she was making the laughing noise so I knew she was having fun. I am always ready to have fun!

After many days Mom stopped using the crutches-sticks, and we walked again. I guess she got smart and figured out they are not fun. I don't know where they went, but they are gone like the kennel. After the crutches-sticks went away, Mom stopped sitting on the stair-steps too. I wish she would still do that so I can lick her face while she makes the laughing noise I love so much.

When we are on walks, I like to find sticks, and I love to stop and spend some time chewing on them. But I can't Lollygag; I have to stay close to Mom and Dad so they don't get lost from me. Mom makes sure I know we don't have time to Lollygag by calling me "Keeper Come."

Joey likes sticks too, but he likes huge sticks. Mom calls them "stick-trees" and makes the laughing noise. Sometimes Joey's stick-trees are so huge I can't get around him on the trail without hitting the tree he is carrying. I like to try to take the trees away, but I am not strong enough to hold them by myself.

Joey is nice and lets me help him carry the big stick-trees. Sometimes I find a stick-tree still in the ground; Joey helps pull hard until we get it out. I like pulling the "still in the ground, trees" and love how Joey helps me. I love Joey so much!

Robbi finds sticks too, and she likes to lay in the trail and chew like me. Mom doesn't let Robbi Lollygag either, so she uses the "Robbi Come" name.

Dad likes to find Christmas trees on the trail; he picks them up and shakes them so I hear and I know he wants to play. Mom and Dad make the laughing noise while we play tug with the Christmas trees.

Jamie Pederson

~ Play ~

*I*t didn't take long for Mom to realize a walk is not enough to make me tired. She noticed I would busy myself by chewing on things I find around the home, and I like attacking too! I attack anything I can, like Joey, Mom and Dad and the furniture. Sometimes when I'm chewing and attacking Mom uses the No-No-No name, and once in a while she names me the "Bad" name. When she uses the "Bad" name I usually get I'm sorry words and extra love-touches, because I am not "Bad," I'm being a puppy.

Toys are so much fun! Sometimes when I find a toy I like, Joey or Robbi will take it away from me. But I don't fret when they take my toys because there are always more to choose from, and we get new ones all the time! I don't think they want the toy; they want to play tug with me. I like the tug game and I'm happy to play anytime they want. I get Joey to play tug sometimes by pushing a toy at him, so I do that a lot.

I love finding things good to chew on like dirty socks, sticks, and shoes! Mom takes them away, but instead of using my No-No-No or Bad name, she gives me something different to chew on. At first, I didn't know what this means, but I learned there are things it is okay for me to chew, and things it is not okay to chew! I still get it wrong sometimes, but I am getting better.

We have a lot of toys that are okay for me to chew, and I can be ornery with them if I want. But when I get the toys just how I like them (all smelly and ripped up), Mom takes them away. I don't know what she is doing with all the toys she takes, but I hope she is saving them to give back as a surprise. Even though she takes my toys away a lot, she is always bringing new ones, so that's good.

Some of our toys make noises when I bite and chew; I like to take the noises out of my toys. Mom calls this "squeak-ectomy!" It is fun to do and Mom isn't using her angry or annoyed voice, so I guess it's okay! After I do a squeak-ectomy Mom takes my toy away and I never get it back. Sometimes Robbi and Joey do the squeak-ectomy; Mom always takes those toys away too.

Now I am bigger and I can attack Joey good. I can get on top of him and chew and I tell him I am the boss. Joey is still a lot bigger than me and sometimes he stands up while I am on his back so I fall off to the floor. When this happens, I bite his legs or jump on his back again. After a while, Joey gets tired and doesn't want to play with me so he sits on me. I don't think that's very nice, and he is being sorry! Mom calls Joey goofball!

Joey is a wonderful big brother; he is always up for some roughhousing, and he doesn't mind when I sneak up and attack him. Sometimes Joey seems to know I am going to jump on him and moves away before I attack. I'm not sure how he knows I'm attacking unless he is cheating with the seeing trick. Mom tells Joey he is silly and makes the laughing noise when I try to jump on him. Mom also makes the laughing noise when I miss, but I think that is mean.

If we don't get enough walks on the trail or field play time, and we have extra energy, Joey plays the yard game with me. I follow Joey out to the grass and we run around in circles as fast as we can, so I can try to catch him.

Sometimes Joey forgets I'm chasing him and he jumps the carefuls in the yard. If I'm following Joey fast and close, I run into the carefuls and get loud hurt. Mom uses angry words telling Joey he is not nice, but I know he doesn't mean to do it. I am one-smart-puppy and I figured out that if Joey does circles in the backyard grass, when we get near the carefuls I turn quickly and make smaller circles. I don't follow him up close anymore. I usually end up running in little circles while Joey runs bigger ones. I haven't been able to catch him yet!

Robbi wants to play with me more now, and sometimes she even helps me attack Joey. One time, when I was being tough and named "Ornery Cuss" with Joey, I attacked Robbi (sometimes I lose where things are when I get excited). I was sure Robbi would be mad and make me go away. But she played back, and we had a great time rolling around.

Now Robbi plays with me a lot, and she even protects me like Joey does! Robbi also lets me snuggle her and sometimes she gives me licks! I'm not surprised because I know I am special and wonderful; it's hard to not love me. Mom tells me this all the time!

I have decided Robbi is awesome and I love her as much as I love Joey. Since Robbi and Joey know where the carefuls are (I never hear them run into stuff), if I stay close to them, I don't get hurt by running into the carefuls so much. They look out for me by pushing me away from carefuls, this is great and Mom calls them the Good name when they do this. I like the Good name!

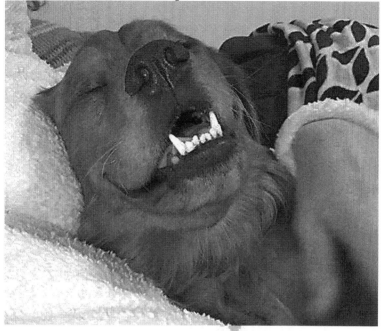

~ Love ~

*M*om tells me I am lucky because I have lots of people who love me. There are lots of people who are lucky because I love them too! I am not choosy about love. I have some special favorite loves though; Mom and Dad are my two most favorite people in the entire world. And there are others I love and I am so excited when I get to smell them.

Grandma and Grandpa are some of my favorite people I love. When they come, they bring their Fur-Kids Copper and Honey. Mom told me Grandma and Grandpa used to be her forever home. When we have

69

visits, the "Moms" make good smelling people food in the kitchen-room. I get lots of tastes because Mom doesn't tell them no very often. I also get lots of love-touches and cuddles. Grandma and Grandpa think I am the bestest most wonderful puppy!

Sister Jeannie is another favorite. She brings little people kids named "Grand" and "Husband Tim." They also name the Grandkids Amaya, Avrey, Abbey and Ajay. When Jeannie and her people come, they are always happy to smell me and give love-touches. Mom makes good smelling people food in the kitchen-room, and I get to play with the Grands. Sometimes they sneak me the people food. Grands are fun to play with, and they don't need rest times like big people do.

Brother Robert is another favorite; he brings Grandkid Landon and Wife Sherry. Robert also has a Fur-Kid named Winston; we get excited when they come to smell us. I get to play with Grand-Landon and Winston Fur-Kid. Winston doesn't always get to come, but when I snuff on Robert, I can smell him. I wish they would always bring Winston because we get to walk the trail or field with them and I like that.

There are also the people called "Friend!" I love Friend-Martina; I first smelled Martina the day I came to my new home. Martina is wonderful! She lives close so we walk to her home for treats. Martina has Fur-Kids, Josie and Indy. We have lots of walks on the trail with them and sometimes we get the field time at a place called school. We spend a lot of time with Martina, Josie, and Indy. They are always happy to smell me and give me touches, loves, and treats.

Martina's Josie is older, and I think she has kids like me somewhere, because she feels like a mother. Josie doesn't get mad when I bump into her and she is always happy and wiggly. She walks slowly, which I like because I get to run around and play more. Sometimes Josie will play tug with me and that is nice.

I like Indy because he is little like Grandma's Fur-Kids. When I try to play with Indy, he growls at me, Mom and Martina tell me to leave him alone or call me No-No-No. What is up with that!? Indy growled at me! I try to leave Indy alone, so he won't growl, but I know if I try hard enough Indy will figure out how cute and wonderful I am. Martina has a little people named Jakub and Husband Randy. They know how cute and wonderful I am and they love me a lot!

Friend-Danette is another favorite people I love! She lives close to us and we walk to her home sometimes too. Danette has a Fur-Kid named Huey. Danette is always happy to smell me and she gives me love-touches and usually gives me treats. I like Huey because he plays rough with me like Joey does. When Huey plays rough Mom and Danette tell him to be careful. I don't understand this careful to Huey, unless they think he will run into me and get hurt. That would be weird because Huey is a lot bigger than me.

Danette and Huey come to smell us and we go walk the trail or have field time with them. Huey has lots of names too, but my favorite is Prince Huey. Joey plays with Huey a lot, but I don't like that because Huey is my friend and Joey takes him away from me. Mom calls me jealous.

Friend-Sue is another favorite people I love! Sue has a Fur-Kid named Hunter and Husband Kelly. We have lots of walks with them. I like to chase Hunter because he runs and runs. When we play this chase and run game, Mom and Sue make the laughing noise I like. Sue does not live close enough to walk for treats, so we take a ride to get there.

Martina, Sue and Danette are some of my favorite people, and they feel like Moms too. They give love-touches, tell me careful and check for Ok-alright. I get the happy-funny inside my tummy when we smell friend people.

When Mom talks about favorite people, she sounds like she has the happy-tummy too. I like happy Mom a lot and wish she was like that all the time. Favorite people and love are the same thing. I hear Mom say love words to all our favorite people, and they say love words back. I can't make the people sound for love, but that's okay because I like the touch for love much better!

Mom tells me about people who love me, but we don't get to smell. These people tell her they love me on [2]Keeper's Tail. She tells me they know how cute and

---

[2] https://m.facebook.com/BlindBabyGolden/

adorable I am. Mom uses a phone to get these words. I don't like it when Mom holds the phone instead of using her hand to touch me, but sometimes she does both and that's okay.

I smell lots of people and Fur-Kids and they seem nice. Mom says I have to be careful because sometimes people are not nice to Fur-Kids, so she tells me No-visit-No-bark. These No-visit-No-bark people don't know how to be nice and I could get hurt from them, so they are carefuls!

Mom said, because I am special, sometimes others don't know how to be nice. I'm not worried because I have so many favorite people who love me and look out for me. They help me know the carefuls; they touch and cuddle and give me treats. I know I am special, wonderful, cute and adorable. Even people-carefuls who don't know how to be nice would love me if Mom would let them smell me. They just don't know how love works!

I try to show everyone how love works, but some people are not very smart about love! Maybe they didn't have a Mom and Dad and a forever home. I am sad for them because love is the most bestest thing ever!

Jamie Pederson

~ Run ~

*O*ne day Mom told Dad "Keeper is a puppy and has too much energy; we need to find a way to let Keeper run." I knew Mom was talking about me because she was using my Keeper name, so I listened. I recognized some words, like "run!" Run is exciting and fun. Run means use all you have inside you to go as fast as you can, stretch your legs and feel the wind in your fur! Run is like taking your happy and excited and pushing it into your legs so it comes out your puppy feet. Run feels like the happy-tummy and the happy laughing sound wrapped up together! Run is also

81

very scary. If you find carefuls when you are running, the HURT words are loud! Not long after Moms "Keeper words" to Dad, we went to a new place. The new place didn't have a trail for my smart-puppy-feet, I wasn't sure where to walk so I would miss the carefuls. When we got to this new place, I got to be off the leash and Mom and Dad walked away from each other. At first it scared me; Mom and Dad need me and I don't want to be away from either of them. I was very worried I would get lost from them. I couldn't stay with them both, so I decided I should stay with Mom.

After we walked away from Dad, I heard him call with loud words "Keeper, Keeper, Keeper, come here Keeper." Since Dad was using his loud voice, I knew he needed me right away! I ran to Dad as fast as I could! While I was running fast, I wasn't thinking about carefuls that might be in the way, all I was thinking is Dad needs me, so I ran! Dad was far away and I was anxious! When I got close Dad said, "You got it, you got it" until I stopped right by his side. I don't know what he needed because he seemed ok, even happy!

Before I could figure out what was going on with Dad, Mom called me "Keeper, Keeper, Keeper, come here

Keeper." I ran fast to Mom, as fast as I could, I wasn't thinking about carefuls. As I was running to Mom, she said loud words "Run Keeper Run, GO-KEEPER-GO." When I got to Mom, she used my Good-Girl name and said, "Did you have fun?"

They called me back and forth many times; soon I understood they were doing this so I could run. I learned they call this new place "field," and "Go-Keeper-Go" is a new game only for me. This new game means Mom and Dad are watching for all the carefuls and throwing words at my ears to tell me there are no carefuls in my way. "Field," "Run," and "Go-Keeper-Go" became some of my favorite things!

When we smell the same trails and fields a lot, I learn the names. One is my favorite because it has a huge

83

field. At this place called Park, I am safe to run because I know where most of the carefuls are. After going to the park a few times, I learned the name "Park," now I get very excited when I hear it because I know I will get to run.

When we go to the park, I don't have to wait for Mom and Dad to go away from each other and call me anymore. I know where to run all by myself. I am so excited when we go to my favorite places that Mom calls me Wiggle Butt! There are other times Mom calls me Wiggle Butt too, usually if I get happy and excited about something.

It feels so good to run and not worry about carefuls. We go to a place so I can run every few days. Robbi doesn't run very much, but Joey loves to run as much as me, so I follow him. Robbi likes to roll around on her back and I run into her sometimes, but she hardly ever gets mad at me anymore.

Sometimes we go to new field places to run; Mom and Dad have to do the walk away from each other and call me so I know it's safe. I don't know how we find all the new fields without carefuls, or how everyone else knows where all the carefuls are. I don't think about it too much, but every once in a while, I wonder how they all know and if I will ever learn.

When we smell the same places, I remember where the carefuls are. As I have gotten bigger and smarter with my puppy-feet, I like to lead the way on these more than one-time trails. Mom tells me it is very impressive how independent I am and names me "Inspiration." I don't know what the new name means, but it sounds good to my puppy ears!

One day while on a walk I could hear water close by, the hot was pushing hard on me so I went to find a drink. I noticed the cool feel of the water on my puppy-feet. I took some steps closer, the water got tall, very fast! Suddenly, I had to do the swimming trick! There was water all around me and I couldn't feel the ground anymore. I was being pushed away from Mom and Dad and it scared me. Mom used loud words "Come Keeper, Come Keeper!" I was trying to "Come Keeper," but Mom's voice was getting away from me and I could tell she was scared too.

Dad was using loud scary words too. I could hear Dad's voice getting closer and then I felt him pick me up out of the water. Dad put me in Mom's arms. Even though I was getting her all watery, she loved and touched me all over, saying you are ok-alright. I was very happy not to be in the tall water anymore. I learned water is a careful because it can get taller fast, and it will take you away!

~ Doctor-Vet ~

*O*ne day Mom took me to a place called "Doctor-Vets," Doctor-Vets has a lot of fur-kid smells, and other smells new to me. I also smelled another of my favorite people named "My-Audrey." There are Doctor people named Doctor-Jackie, Doctor-Christine and Doctor-Mija. I like all the people, but My-Audrey is my favorite! When I get to smell My-Audrey I get so excited I sometimes potty-potty on the floor. My-Audrey doesn't use my No-No-No name or annoyed words.

When we go to the doctor-vet home, I know where My-Audrey is. Mom lets me go by myself because she knows I am smart and I can get there without hitting carefuls. My-Audrey smells so good, like lots of fur-kids; she gives me kisses and treats, and she touches me all over. She gets on the floor with me and she... Oh... I just love her! At the doctor-vet home, Mom uses the No-Pull name because I am excited and I want to get there fast. I have to smell the nice Doctor Ladies too, but I don't mind because they are nice and I like all the love-touches I can get.

After I get love-touches from My-Audrey, we have "Sit-Wait," until they call my name. Doctor Ladies must be popular because there are lots of names called before mine. When they call my name, we go through a door-hole where we have "Sit-Wait" again. I would rather stay with My-Audrey until the Doctor Lady comes, but she has go-to-work.

The Doctor spends a lot of time giving me love-touches. She touches my ears, nose, mouth, and she even lifts my tail to look at the under there part. Mom usually tells me when she will touch these places, but the Doctor Lady must not know she needs to tell me. After touching with her hands, she puts things in my ears and nose to do something called "look." After that she says "checking temperature" and she lifts my tail to put something IN the under-tail part; How Rude!

I'm not sure I like the way Doctor's love, but Mom calls me Good-Girl and says I am Patient. The Doctor Lady does other things, like pet my belly and rub me from my puppy-nose to puppy-feet. She says nice words to Mom that I am healthy, and how cute and adorable I am. I don't know the "healthy" word, but Mom already knows I'm cute and adorable.

Robbi and Joey get to go to the doctor-vet home too, but they don't get as excited about My-Audrey.

~ Yard ~

*A*t home there is a big area for me to play called the yard, to keep me safe there is a fence all the way around it. I bumped into the fence-careful many times. I finally figured out how many puppy-feet steps the fence is from home. Outside the back and front door-holes my feet feel a different touch. These different feels to my feet are called porches. Porches have lots of carefuls called "furniture." I run into furniture-carefuls all the time; just when I think I know where it is, it moves!

When I find furniture-carefuls with my nose or head, Mom says words with her sorry voice. One day Mom got smart and said, "I bought pool noodles and cut them to fit the legs of the furniture." I don't know what the words mean, but if the furniture has legs, that must be why it is always moving. After that, when I hit the furniture it was less hurt and felt softer to my nose and head. But the furniture still moves around.

When I'm in the backyard, I can find the door-hole because my feet feel the different called rug. When I'm in the front yard, there is a step before the door-hole and there is no different feel. I trip on the step a lot because I don't remember where it is.

One day after I tripped on the step, Mom said, "I need to put a rug down so you can feel where the step is." After that, my feet found the same feel-different rug as the back door-hole. The new feel called rug was right in front of the porch step, now my smart-puppy-feet know where the step is. I like rugs because they are fun to chew, but I'm not supposed to chew them or I get the No-No-No name.

There are lots of carefuls in the yard, but most of them never move, so I know where they are and I don't find them the hard way. Sometimes Dad puts a big thing he names "Barbeque" right in the middle of the yard. He makes the barbeque hot and puts food on it. The good smell of food on the barbeque makes me want to see if there are bites. There are usually no bites for me, but it smells good so I have to see if this time he will share.

Dad doesn't tell me when he puts the barbeque-careful in the middle of my play area. I don't like it when I find it with my head or nose. Finding things the hard way causes me hurt and makes Mom upset-sad-sorry! When Dad doesn't tell me about the barbeque, Mom uses loud words at Dad. I don't know why Mom uses loud words; I don't like loud words at all.

Sometimes Mom gets out the long wiggly thing she uses for bath time called hose. She pulls it around the yard to make things watery. The hose is so much fun for me because I get to catch the wiggly thing and play tug with Mom. We did this tug game a lot, until one day when I tugged hard and it made us all watery. After that Mom didn't like to play tug with me and the wiggly water thing anymore. I don't think Mom likes it when the hose gets her all watery.

When Mom puts the hose-careful in the play area, she tells me, "Keeper, be careful." I never know where the hose is because it doesn't stay still. Mom tries to make it easier by saying "careful" at me when I get close. But I still catch it with my feet if she forgets.

Sometimes the hose has a noise and water maker in the middle of the yard called a sprinkler. When the hose connects to the sprinkler, it doesn't move. I like the sprinkler because when the hot is pushing on me I can get close to it and get all watery to cool off.

I am very smart about the carefuls in the home and yard if they don't move. I am good about the carefuls on trails and fields we go to a lot. But I can't figure out carefuls when we are at new places or the carefuls that move. I sure hope I get it soon because I don't like running into them and getting hurt. Mom says I am "One Smart Puppy," so I hope I learn to know like everyone else where they are.

On days when the hot is pushing on me and Mom is the not go-to-work called weekend, we do lots of fun stuff outside the home. Mom spends the whole weekend awake time out in the yard. She plays in the dirt and uses a loud noise to make the grass shorter. I like the smell of grass in my nose when she does this, but I don't like the loud noise it puts in my ears. Mom also puts good smelling stuff called plants in the dirt, but if I try to dig them out, I get the No-No-No name.

One day at home, the hot was pushing on me and making me tired and uncomfortable. I thought it would be nice to do the swimming trick. I was in the backyard grass, using my smart-puppy-feet to find cooler places to lie down. I found a nice cool spot where I didn't feel the hot pushing on me too hard. I decided to take a short sleep. Mom came and said, "Are you hot Keeper?" then she picked me up and carried me to a place in the front yard where she put me in water. I was surprised and confused, but I wasn't mad this time. I wondered where this swimming in the front yard came from. I knew there was no water place at home before!

Mom told me this is a "swimming pool." Swimming pool isn't big enough to move my smart-puppy-feet around like the water at the camping lake. But it is nice and cool and I loved it. Mom showed me how to have water time at the home when the outside is hot and pushing on me hard. I'm so happy I have a Mama to help me learn these things. I hope everyone does.

Some weekends Mom tells us "it's bath time," I don't like bath time and neither do Joey and Robbi! For bath time, Mom brings out the long wiggly hose filled with water and uses it to make us all watery called wet. When we are all watery Mom rubs us with smelly stuff called soap. Soap isn't the good smelly, like dead stuff and poop; soap takes away the good dead and poop smells! Soap takes the good smells off of us too, and soap doesn't taste good.

Mom makes bath time after we have found some good, dead, smelly stuff to roll in and we are happy with how we smell. It's not fair! After bath time, Mom feels bad for taking away our good-dead smell, so she rubs us all over with something that feels good called towel. Then she gives us things to chew called a bully stick or rawhide.

One time after our bath, Mom gave us rawhide (I like rawhide). I don't know why, but she tried to take my rawhide away. I would not let her take my rawhide from me because it was the best thing ever! I showed Mom my teeth and made my most ferocious growl noise at her. I guess that was the wrong thing to do because I got Mom's angry voice and she called me No-No-No and Bad at the same time! Mom had never called me both before, but I didn't want her to take my rawhide. I kept growling and showing my teeth even though Mom was using angry names, but Mom took the rawhide away.

I don't understand why Mom took the rawhide; she gave it back, and then she tried to take it again! I didn't want Mom to take my rawhide again. I didn't like this game at all! I showed Mom my teeth and made my most ferocious growl noise again so she would know I am serious!

Mom called me No-No-No and Bad, and then she took it away. After a while, she gave it back? Mom did this over and over. I was very upset, and I did not like this game!

I stopped growling because I didn't want to be called No-No-No and Bad. Mom gave the rawhide back. I learned if I do not show my teeth and make my most ferocious growl noise when Mom takes it, I will get it back right away. I finally understood Mom was teaching me not to growl at her! Now I let Mom take my rawhide without a growl and I get the Good-Girl name. I also get my rawhide back and she doesn't take it again because I am Good-Girl!

~ Awake Time ~

*I*t didn't take long for me to learn how things work at home. When it's morning, Mom gets morning-cookies to give us while she has coffee and gives me love-touches. On the not-weekend days, Mom and Dad leave for go-to-work after coffee time. While Mom and Dad are at go-to-work we have some short sleeps called a nap, and some play. For the times with no go-to-work, we get the walk called Morning-walk!

On go-to-work days, Mom comes home to eat people food called "lunch." I can smell the lunch-food and I know it is different every time, so I don't know why it's always called lunch. While Mom is home for lunch-food she lets us out the door-hole to potty-potty. After that she gives us a go-to-work cookie, and it's go-to-work again. Dad doesn't come home for the lunch food, so he must get hungry!

After more naps and play, Mom and Dad both come home. Mom spends time in the kitchen-room, making the good smelling food called dinner (which she doesn't share). Mom and Dad eat the dinner-food in the kitchen-room, or sometimes in the couch-room while they have "be-quite-I'm-watching-TV".

When the dinner food is gone, Mom or Dad put all the stuff that still has a little food left on it in the dishwasher. They do the dishwasher thing so I can lick off some food; it is very nice of them to do this for me.

When I finish helping with the dishwasher food, we get our collars and leashes on for walk-the-trail or field-time. I don't know how Mom and Dad know whether we do field or trail each day, but I am happy either way.

We go places with different names like home-trail, school-field and park-field. Walks are always with Mom and Dad and sometimes with other people too. I like walking with other people and Fur-Kids. We often walk with Martina, Josie, and Indy, or Sue, Hunter, and sometimes Gunner. There are not-as-often people too, like Jeannie and the Grands, or Robert, Sherry, Landon, and Winston.

Sometimes we have no-walk time! These no-walks happen when we are doing other fun things, or when Mom and Dad are too tired or feel not-so-good. When we have no-walk, I try to play with Joey more or run around the backyard all by myself. I like walk time much better than no-walk!

We have lots of favorite walk places. Sometimes we go in the car-truck, but lots of times we walk the trail right from home. The trail by home is easy for me because I know most of the carefuls, and I like that I get to lead the way. The not-at-home trails are lots of fun, but I have to listen good for Mom and Dad to warn me about carefuls.

After walking or field time, we usually do stuff at home. Joey and I play a lot, and sometimes Robbi too, but she mostly barks at us. Dad usually sits in the couch-room and listens to people I can't smell and who are not in the home. Sometimes I bark at the not-here people, but Dad says, "Be quiet I'm trying to watch TV." I still don't understand these words.

For at-home-time Mom likes to play outside or sit in the couch-room with her phone or iPad. When Mom has couch-room time I get to lay with my head in her lap while she love-touches me. Sometimes Mom tells me what the people on the Facebook Page Keeper's Tail say. I like home-time because Mom and Dad are both at home and I don't have to worry about when they will come back. When it's go-to-work or you-can't-go times, sometimes I get worried they won't come home; I need them to come home!

Other things happen during home awake time, but not every day. Mom pushes something around on the floor that makes a loud noise; they call this vacuuming. I don't know why Mom does the vacuuming, but she moves all our toys to the toy box first. I don't like the vacuuming because I have to keep moving out of the way. Sometimes I chase the noise maker and bark at it to let it know I want it to stop. When I do, Mom makes the laughing noise. Mom also does sweep-mop; it's like vacuuming except it doesn't make the loud noise. I like sweep-mop better because I get to chase and bark at it; I let it know I am the boss!

105

For nighttime, we all go to the up-steps part of the home for big-fluffy-soft-bed sleep. This is where we stay until the next awake time. Sometimes the night is too long of sleep for me and I need to Potty-potty. Mom or Dad opens the door-hole and let me go to the yard for potty-potty. After I "finish-my-business" we go back to the big-fluffy-bed.

In the night time on the big-fluffy-bed, Mom and Dad sleep too. I lay on the bed next to Mom or Dad so I can feel them close. If they don't feel really close, I find where they are and lay next to them again. Sometimes I have to move lots of times to be close. I don't know why they move away, but I need to feel them close so I can sleep too.

When it is sleep-time Joey doesn't like to be touched. If I touch him when I am trying to find Mom or Dad, he growls at me; I don't sleep next to Joey so he won't growl at me. Robbi hardly ever does night sleep-time on the bed; she usually sleeps on the floor. Sometimes Mom calls Robbi to the bed using the Robbi-come name. When she does, I try to get there first so I can get the love-touches. Mom names me Brat when I do this.

When outside the home is warm on me, we spend more awake-time in the yard. If Mom or Dad is home, the door-holes are always open and I can go out whenever I want. When the outside the home is cold on me, we have shorter walks, and the door-holes are closed. Closed means I have to ask if I want to go outside. Asking to go outside is easy; I go to where the door-hole is and sit there until I hear the opening noise. If I don't hear the opening noise, I use my smart-puppy-feet and hit the door, or I whine, so someone knows I am waiting.

I don't know how to make the opening noise, and I can only ask to go out when Mom or Dad is home to make the noise for me. Sometimes we get the doggie-door-hole. With the doggie-door-hole I can go out whenever I want. Mom and Dad never give us the doggie-door-hole when they are not at home. If I could make people's words, I would tell them we would like them to leave the doggie-door-hole for us to use.

Jamie Pederson

~ Treats ~

I like treat and cookie time; Mom gives us cookies when she leaves for go-to-work and you-can't-go. When Mom does cookie time, she tells us she is leaving and asks if we want a cookie. I always want cookies so I find Mom (she is usually standing by the cookie place), and I sit with my mouth in the air. Mom named this my baby bird face and says I look like a hungry little bird. I wait for my cookie, I know it's my turn when Mom says "one for Keeper," and then I feel it by my nose. I have to "be-nice" which means not

109

bite Mom's fingers. Sometimes if I am excited or if I'm worried someone will take mine, I get "grabby" and bite Mom's finger. I never mean to bite and when I do Mom yelps a little to let me know she has hurt, but she doesn't get mad.

I learned "go-to-work cookie" means Mom is leaving and I don't get to go. I tried to tell her I would rather go than have a cookie by refusing to take the cookie. Mom said she "Sorry," then she gave me love-touches on my head and said "Keeper can't go." I learned that not taking the cookie doesn't mean I get to go. Now when Mom offers me a cookie, I take it even though I would rather go.

When other people who are not Mom and Dad give cookies, it's called "treat time!" Other people don't always know how it works for me. Even though I put my face in the air and I am ready for treats, they forget to tell me "one for Keeper," or "here Keeper." If I don't hear the words and get to feel it by my nose, I have to find the treat, which is hard. Sometimes other people don't understand that I know how to "be-nice." I think they are afraid I will bite their fingers. Treat time is always a little harder than cookie time with Mom, but I still like it a lot! I have to work a little harder to find the treat.

~ What's Best ~

When I first came to the home, I was little and I couldn't walk very far without getting tired. For long walks, Mom or Dad would carry me or put me in a ride called a wagon. The wagon is like the car-truck because you sit in it and it goes. When Mom put me in the wagon, sometimes I didn't like it because I wanted

113

to walk. I tried to tell her by barking and whining. When I barked and whined Mom said, "I promise I will always do what is best for you." I didn't understand the words, but I learned I do not like what's best-for-you stuff.

For one best-for-you Mom said, "Keeper, you are getting too heavy for me to carry upstairs for bedtime. It is time for you to learn stairs." Learning stair-steps was scary and very hard; it was no fun at all. Joey tried to help. I heard noises of him running up and down and sometimes he stopped to poke at me with his nose. But I wasn't having it! I did not understand why Mom was being so mean. I knew Mom loved to pick me up and snuggle while she carries me! But Mom was very stubborn, and she said, "Keeper, it is best-for-you."

Mom loves me a lot, and she knows I don't like learning new things. She tried to help me by putting me at the bottom step and naming at me "Keeper you can do it"! Following Mom's voice, one step at a time, I went up. Mom stayed right by my side and made sure I knew she was there. It didn't take long until I was at the top and Mom was so happy. Going up the stair-steps wasn't bad, I got it right away.

Then it was time for me to go down the stair-steps; down was very scary, I was sure I would fall and get hurt. Mom promised I was safe and she would stay close. But I thought it was one of those times Mom was being sorry. I knew if I waited long enough Mom would realize this was not smart for me. Mom tried naming "Come Keeper" at me, then Dad named at me too; they both tried for a long time. Since Mom is always the one who takes care of these things, I didn't trust that Dad wasn't being sorry too. I showed them how stubborn I am, and I refused.

They finally realized I wasn't having it, so Mom brought some of my favorite treats. Mom said if I would take one step I could have treats! But I am not a fool; I refused even though I wanted the treat. For a long time, I sat on the stair-steps and whined, trying to tell Mom she is wrong, that stair-steps are scary and hard!

Didn't Mom realize I am a little puppy, and I needed taken care of? Mom did not give up. She stayed right there, loving and touching me. She said encouraging words and even helped a little. I finally went down one step and WOW, Mom really liked that! I couldn't believe how happy I made Mom with one tiny step! I like the happy Mom so I went down another step, and another, and she was so excited!

Okay, stair-steps are not as scary as I thought. So slowly… feeling with my smart-puppy-feet… one careful step at a time… I went all the way down…until I was at the bottom, no more steps!

WOW! I made it all the way to the last step! How great is that! I was so happy with myself that I ran right… back… up…!

Well, I had not thought THAT through; now I was back at the top and I had to come down the stair-steps again. I knew Mom would make me come down on my own because now she knew I could. I was right, Mom named at me to come back down. Maybe Mama is not the only sorry one here; I guess I have a little sorry too!

Once I got used to going down the stair-steps, it wasn't so bad. I also like that I don't have to wait for Mom to carry me up for nighttime. Now I am bigger and smarter. I go up to the bed any time I want. I am good at stair-steps now, sometimes I run up and down for fun, and sometimes Joey chases me up and down the stairs. Mom doesn't like it when we run on the stair-steps and she uses loud words to tell us "someone will get hurt!" but I don't know who this someone is.

When Mom and Dad go up and down the stairs, I like to chase them and bite their feet and leg sleeves. When I do, they use my No-No-No name and say, "Keeper, someone will get hurt." I want to meet this "Someone" and tell them to be more careful so I can do fun things.

When I learned the stair-steps, I understood that best-for-you doesn't mean it's easy, but it can be lots of good for me. Does everyone have to do what's best-for-you; and if everyone does, how do they stop being afraid? I can smell when people are afraid sometimes. Maybe they are afraid because they are learning something scary and best-for-you.

Another best-for-you was learning to use the doggie-door-hole. This sounded silly since doggies are not doors. But the doggie-door-hole is awesome! Before, we had to wait for the opening-the-door-hole noise to go to the backyard. But the doggie-door-hole made a way for us to go in the backyard through a flap I pushed open with my nose. I heard Joey and Robbi use it a few times, but I was not sure this was right for me.

The hole is small and to go through I have to lift my smart-puppy-feet and jump a little. Jumping through the doggie-door-hole was very scary for me. I wasn't sure there is a ground on the other side to catch me. If I can't feel my next step with my foot, how do I know I won't fall a long way and get hurt?

Mom tried for a while to get me to step through to go outside. When that didn't work, she tried to show me by taking me outside and calling me to come inside. Mom pushed and pulled the flap while she held a treat in her hand. She did this a lot, so I learned not to be afraid of the noise it makes. After I wasn't afraid of the noise, she offered the treat if I went through. I tried so I could get the treat. Using the door-hole the first time was scary. After the first time it was easy because I knew there was ground to catch me. I got to show Mom how smart and brave I am, and now I can go outside whenever I want.

After lots of days, the outside pushed cold on me and the doggie door-hole was gone. I hope they find it soon; I don't want to forget how to use it. I don't know how something as big as a doggie door-hole could just be gone! For now, I have to ask to go outside again. Mom and Dad don't always notice I am waiting, so I wait and whine or bark until they do.

When the outside the home was pushing warm again, Mom found the doggie door-hole. It is a very wonderful thing because I get to go out as much as I want. I don't understand why the doggie door-hole is gone sometimes, or why it's always gone at the bed-sleep and you-can't-go times. I wish I could make people's word noises to tell Mom I like having the doggie door-hole. She should leave it all the time, even when the outside is pushing cold and watery.

When I was still a little puppy, I got to sit on Mom's lap for rides in the car-truck. After I got bigger, I rode with Robbi and Joey in a different part, like a big kennel. Learning to get in and out of the car-truck kennel was hard and scary for me. The door-hole of the kennel is high over my head and I am not sure how high to jump. Dad fixed this scare for me by making stair-steps like in the home. Dad put the new stair-steps on the car-truck kennel. The next best-for-you I learned was how to use the stair-steps for the car-truck kennel.

The inside of the car-truck kennel is nice and cozy like a go-to-work kennel. I am always excited to go down the stair-steps as soon as the door-hole opens, so I can find what fun we will do. But I have a very hard time going up. Mom said "Keeper, don't worry, you will get it soon, you are one Smart Puppy." I'm not so sure I will ever be able to do the going up, because going up makes me scared. For now, they help me by lifting on my fluffy butt. I'm so glad I have a Mom and Dad!

~ Listen ~

*O*ne day before I learned to love the water, we went to the place called the river. Joey and Robbi were getting all watery and I was on the not-water-part with Mom. I was whining because I couldn't get to Robbi and Joey without getting all watery. I don't like it when they are where I can't feel them close by.

Mom said, "Keeper, Listen." When Mom says words to my ears using my Keeper name, I try to catch them, so I waited for more. She said "Listen" again and my ears caught a thud sound close by. I went to the sound and found a stick with Moms smell on it. Mom had lost the stick, and she was asking me to help, so I picked up the stick and took it to her. I must have been right because she was happy to get that stick back.

Mom said, "Keeper, listen" again and my ears heard the same sound. I went to the sound and again I found the stick! Mom was so excited the first time. I was sure I did the right thing when I brought the stick back. What was going on? I took Moms stick back to her again, and she named me Good-Girl. Right away, I heard the "Thud," and the stick was far away again. We did this a few more times and Mom was happy each time I brought the stick to her. Mom said this is fetching; but I name it the listen game.

Sometimes on walks Mom uses the listen game for me to find Dad; I know when Mom says, "Keeper, Listen, where is Daddy?" I am supposed to find him. Dad usually helps me by throwing loud words at my ears. This is a lot like "Go-Keeper-Go" but I don't know we are playing until Mom says "Keeper, listen." Sometimes Mom says "Keeper, listen, where's Robbi and Joey?" this is harder because they don't always help me by making noise, I can only find them if they make noise.

One day Mom said, "Keeper, I got you a new toy." These words mean something new for me to play with. She said, "This toy is for the listen game." Then she said, "Keeper, sit, listen," I heard a new sound. This sound was like a people kid laughing. I tried to take the new toy from Mom, but the laughing noise went across the yard and my ears heard it far away! Finding this toy was easy because it was still making noise at my ears. When I found the new toy, Mom was calling me so I took it to her.

I didn't want to give Mom my new toy, but she took it away from me and said, "Good-Girl, Keeper is one smart Puppy." I was sad because she took my new toy, and then the laughing noise went far away again. I found it and brought it back. Mom called this fetching too. We did this fetching many times. Since the sounds keep going, it helps me find the toy, and the game is so much better! Mom has other listen-fetch-bring toys too, but I like the laughing noise the best.

When we go to the field or walk, Mom and Dad play a game with Joey called "Ball," "Bring it," or "Fetch." I am not sure how the game works, but I hear a noise go across the field where there are no carefuls. Joey's noisemaker-ball is not loud. It goes much farther away, and it doesn't keep making noise for Joey; he has to use his nose-smeller. Joey runs after the noise and brings it back again and again. It's a lot like my listen game, but Joey does it so I can run, and we get to run a lot! Joey gives the noisemaker-ball back to Mom or Dad each time. I bark a lot to tell them to send it away again so we can run and find it. I like Joey's "Ball, Bring it, Fetch" better than my listen game because Joey does all the work and I get to run! It is nice of Joey to do this for me, I love him so much!

Sometimes on walks I lose where Mom is, because I get too far away. I don't like losing her, but she always knows where I am. If I lose her, I play the listen game. I stop and put my ears up and stand very still until I hear Mom say, "I'm right here Keeper." Now I know right where to go to find Mom again. I don't like it when I don't know where Mom is so I'm glad she always knows where I am.

~ Camping ~

I love Camping; camping means no go-to-work, and I'm with Mom and Dad all the time! We do lots of fun new things and have long walks called hikes. Mom loads all our favorite toys and blankets into a tiny home that moves like the car-truck. When all the important overnight home stuff is in the tiny moving home, called motor home, we go through the door-hole and have a long ride. When we stop riding, we are at a place called "The Property." The motor home has all the same things as the forever home and it smells like Mom and Dad and Joey and Robbi. I explored around inside and even found a big fluffy bed! When it is sleep-time, we all have long sleep-time on the bed in the motor home; this is Camping.

In the morning, we go out the door-hole and there are lots of people who come camping and to love me. Some of these camping people I already know. But some I smell for the first time; they all love-touch me and feed me lots of good food I don't usually get to have. Camping is lots of days and nights without going to the forever home, and there is no go-to-work, or you-can't-go times. Camping is my favorite!

The first camping we did was for my Happy Birthday Three Months. While we were camping, we went from The Property for a short car-truck ride. When the ride was over, we got out of the car-truck and into a boat. At first, the boat scared me a lot because it is loud and moves around making it hard for me to stand.

I stayed in Mom's lap and pushed my ears on her so I wouldn't be so scared. After a while, the loud boat noise stopped. Mom picked me up, and she dropped me in the water! What the heck was Mom thinking?! She didn't ask me if I wanted to go in the water; she dropped me in! That was not nice at all!

I learned the new trick called swimming! At first, it scared me because I didn't know what to do. I learned I could move around in the water with my smart-puppy-feet and this helped keep my head out of the water. This is the swimming trick! The cool water was nice since the hot was pushing on me that day, but I didn't let Mom know that I liked it. I let Mom think I was mad at her for a while.

We do the swimming trick a lot when the air outside is hot, but we don't always go to the swimming place in the boat. Sometimes we have swimming in the creek right at the camping place. Or we go in the car-truck to the place called lake and put chairs and blankets on the ground by the water.

When we go to the lake, Mom brings floater toys to put in the water. She calls them paddle board and kayak. Mom uses the floater toys to go out on the water and leaves me behind. I do not like being left behind, so I ran into the water and did the swimming trick to get to her. Mom wasn't mad. She was making the laughing sound and helped me onto the floater toy with her. We stayed on the floater and moved around in the water for a long time.

Now when Mom plays with her floater toys, I get to ride on them too. Sometimes I get to go with Dad or other people for float playtime. I am good at knowing when the floater toys are there. If anyone goes, I run fast and get on, so they can't leave me behind!

One day Dad took all of us Fur-Kids in his water floater drift boat. Mom went with us in the car-truck, but she wasn't in the boat with us. I could hear the water hitting the side of the boat, and I could feel the moving that means we were on the water. We floated around for a while and then I heard Dad throwing loud words like he was talking to someone far away. When Dad stopped making words, I heard Mom throw words back from far away. I do NOT like Mom far away from me, so I jumped out of the drift boat into the water!

At first it scared me because my head went under. When my head came up, I heard Mom sending loud words in her scared voice "Keeper, Keeper, come to Mama Keeper." I did the swimming trick to where Mom was on her floater kayak and she helped me get with her. Mom sounded scared, and she kept checking me for Ok-alright. After Mom checked me all over, she made the laughing noise and I stayed with Mom until we went back to the car-truck.

Now when we go to the water, Mom makes me wear a new coat called "float-coat" or "life-jacket." With this coat, I stay on top of the water even if I'm not moving my puppy-feet. I don't like the float-coat because it wraps all around me, but Mom said it's one of those best-for-you things!

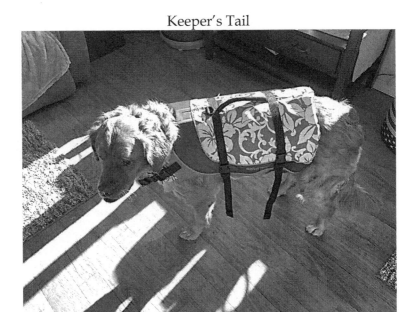

When we are camping and the air outside is cold, we do a campfire in the middle of the grass area. Campfire is very hot and people like to sit close; they put good-people-food close to it too. When I try to get a taste of food close to the campfire, it is too hot for me and I can't get close enough. When I feel the hot, Mom uses loud words "Keeper, be careful, Hot!" Silly Mom, I can feel the "Hot" and I know it is a careful!

When camping is over, the motor home moves like a car-truck. After another long ride we go out the door-hole and we are back at the forever home. I'm not sure why we do the camping, but I like it.

~ Happy Birthdays ~

$\mathcal{M}$om likes to tell me "Happy Birthday," she sings and gets excited. Singing is like talking, but it feels different to my ears. When you sing, you throw loud, happy words to everyone. I like it when Mom sings because it makes me feel the good in my tummy!

My Happy Birthdays are two months, three months, four months... Mom always tells me "Happy Birthday Keeper, you are getting so big!" So, it has something to do with that.

Robbi and Joey have Happy Birthday too, Robbi was Happy Birthday 8 years, and Joey was Happy Birthday 2 years. I know I am special because mine are months and I have a lot more of them. I learned there are Happy Birthday years for people too. Everyone has them! For every Happy Birthday, we get special treats and extra toys. We all get the treats and toys, even if it is my Happy Birthday, or Robbi or Joey's.

When Dad had his Happy Birthday, we were vacation-camping, and there were lots of people. We had so many people and Fur-Kids I can't remember all the names; I don't even know if I got to smell them all. The people were singing, yelling, and laughing. Everyone was walking and running and talking to everyone else. People put food down all over the camping place so I could taste it. Sometimes no one said anything when I had a taste, but other times they used my No-No-No name. I don't know why people would put food down for me and then use my No-No-No name.

When it was sleep-time some people left, but some stayed and they put big rooms called "tent" all over the grass area. I bumped into the tents a lot, but they were soft and didn't make me hurt. The camp people had long sleep time in the tent rooms when we went to the motor home.

There are other days like Happy Birthday. Some are Thanksgiving, Independence Day, Labor Day, and Merry Christmas Day. They also call these "holidays". They are like Happy Birthday because we have lots of people around and lots of good food smells. For the holidays, there are sometimes new toys for me. I like new toys! We do holidays at camp or at home; and sometimes we go to other people's homes. I like it a lot.

For the special Merry Christmas holiday, Mom put an outside tree inside the house. Silly Mom! She took me to where she put the tree so I could touch it, know where it is, and not run into it. For this holiday, Mom put a Merry Christmas sweater on me even though I was inside and the cold wasn't pushing on me. She put a Merry Christmas sweater on Robbi and Joey too, so the cold must have been pushing on her. I didn't like the sweaters at all; I hope she never does it again!

For Merry Christmas, we got lots of toys, but they had paper all over them and we had to take the paper off to play with them. Everyone who came to our home brought us toys inside paper! People told us we were cute with our sweaters and they said love words and gave love-touches. The people felt sad for me because I had to wear the sweater so they brought toys to make me feel better. I guess it's ok to wear a Merry Christmas sweater if it means we get lots of loves and toys.

~ Snow ~

One day Mom said, "Happy Birthday 9 Months Keeper; I have a surprise for you." I heard the opening-the-door sound and when I ran outside there was cold stuff all over the ground. Snow! At first, I was nervous because the snow was new. Robbi and Joey were excited and ran into the yard to roll in the snow, and then Joey was running fast circles. I went outside with careful steps to check it out. I decided

145

right away; I LOVE SNOW too! I ran and rolled and jumped and buried my face. Snow is wonderful stuff! I want this snow surprise every day! Mom said, "Today is also Robbi's Happy Birthday 8 years" and she did the Happy Birthday singing! I don't know how she made snow, but it is way better than new toys!

Snow covered the ground and everything outside the home for days. It was hard for my smart-puppy-feet to know where the carefuls are, so I had to be extra smart with my puppy-feet. All the smells were underneath the snow. When I am not sure where carefuls are, I lift my feet tall. This way I can feel the carefuls with my feet before I find them with my nose causing hurt. When I do careful walking, Mom says I look like a "Tennessee Walker" and she makes the laughing noise!

We went on the trail and to the field to play in the snow. We got to play with Huey, and Josie and Indy in the cold fluffy snow all day. The snow made everything have less noise to my ears. It was heavy and stuck to my fur, so sometimes it pulled when I moved which didn't feel good, but I like it anyway. Mom tried to help by putting smelly stuff on my feet called coconut oil. It tasted good, but I wasn't sure why she put it on my feet.

After a while, I noticed snow wasn't sticking where the smelly coconut oil was. Mom didn't put coconut oil on my legs and tummy and they had lots of snow on them. Maybe next time Mom will put coconut oil all over me.

Walking in the snow is hard; I learned to walk where the snow is not soft and fluffy but hard to my feet called "packed." My feet helped me know where to step on the hard snow, the same as feeling the trail so I don't run into carefuls! I am fast learning and I soon knew to step on packed snow and I could go fast. Joey and Robbi seemed to know where to go. I still can't figure out how they know all the carefuls. I hope I learn soon.

After some days, there was no more snow. I am not sure where it went, but the next time we went on walks I had to learn about new carefuls called "Over." Over-carefuls are because trees broke in the snow. Now I have to crawl over the top of the tree because we cannot careful around them. The overs are all different, so Mom had to help me know the right place to do the over trick.

There is also a new careful called "Under." Under-carefuls are like overs, but with space on the bottom, Mom showed me where to do the under trick too. For "under" you have to scrunch yourself small, so you don't hit them. Sometimes an "over" for Joey and Robbi is an "under" for me. This is because Robbi and Joey have taller legs and can get over easier. We had the "over" and "under" carefuls for a while, and then they were gone.

~ Beaches ~

*O*ne day we went for a long ride in the car-truck, the ride was so long I was getting worried about potty-potty. Mom must have known I had to potty-potty because we finally stopped. But just to do our business and then back in the car-truck for another long time. When we stopped again, Sister Jeannie, the Grands and Husband-Tim were there too.

We went down lots of steps like the stair-steps at home. When we got to no-more-steps, the ground felt

151

different to my puppy-feet. I was not sure about this place, so I walked with tall, careful steps. We went through some short water; it only came to my tummy, so I didn't have to do the swimming trick. I was nervous about crossing the water because I learned you don't know when it would get tall. But Mom and Dad told me, "Keeper, it's okay." After we crossed the short water Mom said, "It's OK Keeper, you can run." Oh, these are some of my favorite words!

The different feeling ground is called sand, and the place we were at is called the beach. There was a loud roaring noise coming to my ears from all around us, and the air had the taste named salty. We spent the whole day running in the sand and running away from the water called waves. The water at the beach is different than the swimming-trick-water at the camping-lake. And it had the taste named salty too.

We crawled over rocks, which is hard for me because they are lots of carefuls bunched up together. Everyone helped me know where to put my puppy-feet, and I had so much fun. There were lots of new and different smells and tastes that day. I got to smell new people, who told Mom how cute and adorable I am. We ran and played, and we found lots of little stuff called shells in the sand; Mom took them home because she liked them.

Running in the sand and water-waves is my favorite. I learned there are no carefuls in the sand, and sometimes the water-waves sneak up and get me. Joey played the "fetch-bring" game with sticks so I could help. Everyone had fun; we ate food and climbed on rocks, ran in the sand and played in the water all day. I like the Beach!

We went to the beach again, but with Martina, her people and Fur-Kids. They still called it the Beach, but it was different because there were no stairs and no big rocks. I like this Beach too, and it was fun to have other fur-kid friends along. Robbi and Joey like to run and run on the beach and I get to chase them. I know they are chasing because of how they run, but I don't know what they are chasing.

We went to the beach again with Danette and Huey. Danette brought new friends Kyle and Kaitlyn and Fur-Kid Maggie. I followed Joey and Robbi in the water-waves and I learned the noises they were chasing are called birds. Mom and Dad walked a long time in the sand, so I ran around them and barked.

Sometimes the water-waves would sneak up and get me and everyone made the laughing noise. At this Beach Mom picked up round things called sand dollars that tasted funny. She also picked up rocks and other stuff to take home. Every time we go to the beach, I have so much fun and I can't wait to go again.

Sometimes we go to a beach called "The River." River-beaches don't have a long-drive, and the water is not salty. The water-waves don't come get me, and the noise is different to my ears. The feel is different to my feet, and the smell is different to my nose. The sand is still good and there are no carefuls. When we go to any beach, we always take friends or we smell them when we get there. Friends are part of why I like the beach so much. I like friends a lot!

Jamie Pederson

~ Mom's Hurt ~

When I was still little something scary was going on with Mom; I could smell something scared her. Mom would go away, but not go-to-work. When she came home, she smelled like the doctor-vet place, but without animal smells. She had salty water on her face that meant she was sad, so I gave her extra love-touches.

One day Mom went away for a long, long time; longer than ever before! I worried she wouldn't come back home. While she was away, we had visits from Robert and Danette so we could potty-potty and play a little, but no Mom or Dad. Finally, Mom came home, and it was already sleep time! I was very happy to have her home, and I snuffed all over her. She smelled like the doctor-vet place without the animal smell again.

When she came home this time Mom was different. She didn't smell scared anymore. I knew She was tired, and she hurt, but she was happy like after a bath when you're glad it is over. I made her feel better by staying close to her to snuggle and love. Mom told me I was sweet, and she loved me so much. Mom went right to the bed. I was very sad she had hurt, but I was so happy she was home! I went to the bed to be with her and snuggle and love her.

For lots of days Mom was having hurt. Sister Jeannie came for a visit each day. She took Robbi, Joey and me down the trail while Mom rested. I didn't want to leave her because I knew she hurt and needed me; but she said, "It's OK Keeper, have fun." Mom was tired!

Some days Mom would leave by herself and when she came back, she would take a nap. Mom doesn't do the sleep-time called a nap, so it worried me. She said, "I am going for walks without you because I am trying to get better." I didn't like it at all because I always make Mom feel better, so she needed to take me too!

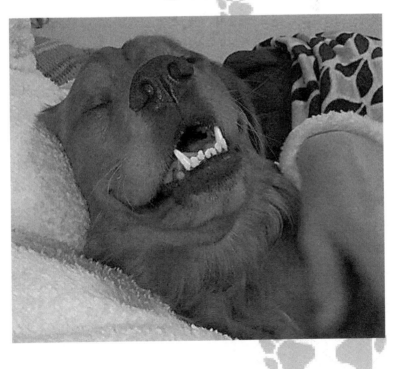

Grandma, Martina, and Danette all came to smell us while Mom was trying to get better. But they didn't bring their Fur-Kids. Mom's hurt worried them, and they wanted to help her feel better too. Mom said it isn't vacation or weekend, but she stayed home anyway with no go-to-work. Dad stayed home for some days too, but he had the "go-to-work" sooner than Mom.

After a lot of days Mom seemed better, so she walked with us again. She was slow and got tired fast. After more days Mom was more like she used to be, not always tired and hurt. I am very happy she is the way she used to be; the tired, hurt Mom worried me a lot!

~ Hero Keeper ~

$\mathcal{M}$om was still home for her hurt and didn't have the "go-to-work" yet, when I had hurt and a hard time breathing. When I don't feel good, I stay close to Mom and push on her so she will make it better. Mom felt bad for me, so she took me to see My-Audrey at the doctor-vet home. My-Audrey always helps me feel better, and everyone there gives me love-touches.

I spent smelling time with the Doctor-Lady, because she knows how wonderful I am and loves me so

163

much. She poked around on my nose; it didn't feel good, but I let her. I don't know why she would put hurt on me if she likes me, but Mom said this is another best-for-you. The Doctor-Lady told Mom words, infection and antibiotics, but I don't know these words. After she did her poking at me, I got to play with My-Audrey more and we went home.

Mom gave me medicine wrapped in cheese. I like cheese! I felt better in my nose, but bad inside my tummy. After a few days, my tummy was feeling terrible. The cheese came back out my mouth in an icky way called throwing up, so Mom stopped giving me medicine. We went back to smell My-Audrey. This time Doctor-Mija wanted to smell and love-touch on me. I let her poke around my nose a little and it didn't hurt as much. She said "wait and see," which I decided means do nothing. I got to play with My-Audrey again so that was good.

Some days later, the top of my nose hurt again, so Mom took me back to the doctor-vet home. I spent some time with Doctor- Jackie and she cleaned my nose good, (which I didn't like). She told Mom she might fix my nose when I came in to be spayed. I tried to let Mom know I wanted to go play with My-Audrey again and we did.

Later, Mom took me to a place that smelled like the doctor-vet home. The people were nice, but My-Audrey wasn't there, this made me sad. At the new "no-My-Audrey" place was Doctor-Man-Roberto. We smelled Doctor-Roberto, and he love-touched me and checked my nose. He was very nice, and he liked me a lot. There were lots of other nice people who wanted to smell me too. I didn't like being in a place that smelled like My-Audrey's place, but didn't have My-Audrey.

Doctor- Roberto told Mom new words, "CAT Scan." I know about cats, they smell funny, so I figured this is what's wrong with my nose. I don't remember smelling a cat, so it confused me. Doctor- Roberto also said a surgery word. I am not sure about the surgery word. I think it means sweet because it sounds like the word Mom uses if I find fruit and candy. But whatever they had that was surgery they didn't share with me. That's all we did so I think we went because Doctor-Roberto needed what Mom names "Keeper love."

After more days, Mom took me back to the place with Doctor-Roberto. I could smell Mom was scared, and she had salty water on her face so I didn't like being there at all this time. Doctor-Roberto told Mom to let me go away from her with the nice girls. It was very hard for me to go because Mom had salty water on her face, which means she needs me to love and cuddle so she will be Ok-alright.

The nice girls put me in a place that felt like the go-to-work kennel. I tried to tell them I know potty-potty, and they would not have to name me No-No-No if they let me out. But they didn't listen and left me there for a long time! The girls came to smell and love-touch me sometimes, but I was all alone like the go-to-work kennel, but without Joey close by. After a while, one of the nice girls poked me with something sharp, which I didn't think was nice. I got tired, and I went to sleep.

When I woke up, Mom was in the kennel with me. She was giving me love-touches and cookies and telling me I am such a Good-Girl and she is so proud of me. I know Mom uses the proud name for Joey because he is a hero, so maybe I am a hero now too.

Mom took me home; I was tired and my inside tummy felt the not good kind of funny. While I was resting on Mom's lap, I heard her tell Dad "They didn't do the surgery; they found a cyst during the CAT scan. I'm taking her back in a week." I don't know these words; there was no sweet like candy and I didn't smell a cat. Mom wasn't feeling good too, and she didn't know what she was saying.

Some days later, Mom took me back to Doctor-Roberto. I could smell it scared Mom, and she had salty water on her face again. I decided I don't like this place because it makes Mama scared-sad-worried. Mom told me, "Keeper, Mama loves you so much, it's okay, you're a Good-Girl." I don't know why Mom goes to this doctor-vet if it makes her scared-sad-worried. Why do they make her let me go with the nice girls when she needs me the most?

This time was the same as before. The girls put me in the not go-to-work kennel and they wouldn't listen when I told them I know potty-potty. They told me everything would be Ok-alright, but I worried about Mom. After I woke up this time, Mom and Martina were both in the kennel with me. They told me I am such a Good-Girl and I would be Ok-alright. Mama said she is proud of me again, so I decided I am a hero too! If this is a hero, I'm not sure I like it though!

I don't know why Mom worried about my Ok-alright; it was Mama that needed Ok-alright. Mom had salty water on her face again. But she seemed different and kind of happy; like the after you get your ears cleaned and you're glad it's over, happy. Mom was happy because she could be with me and that makes me a hero. If helping Mama be Ok-alright makes me a hero, I am the biggest hero ever!

I was very tired and the top of my mouth hurt. But I could breathe better and there was a different feeling inside my head, like not pushing. After some love-touches I went back to sleep. When I woke up again, I was still in the go-to-work kennel, but Mom and Martina were not there. I was still tired, so I had another sleep that was long and felt like a fluffy bed sleep. When I woke up the next time, one of the nice girls took me to Mom and we went home.

When we got home Robbi and Joey snuffed all over me and spent lots of time checking me for hurt. They didn't seem worried about Mom, so it's a good thing she has me! My mouth hurt for a few days, but Mom was happy again. When Mom is Ok-alright, it makes me feel good too!

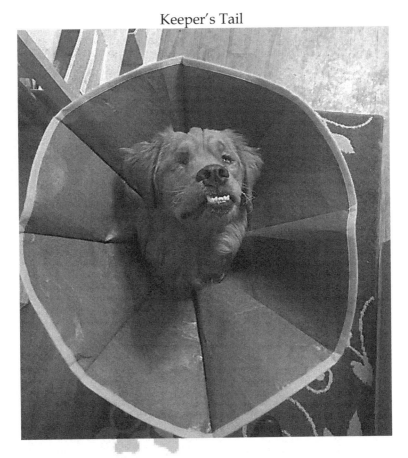

~ Little Flower ~

*W*hen Mom said we were going to the doctor-vet again, I was happy because I would get to smell My-Audrey. This time Mom left me at the Doctor-lady place all by myself and I spent the whole day! She had never done this before, but I wasn't worried because I was with all the nice people who love me. Mom told me I would be spayed, I remember hearing the word "spayed" before, but don't know what it means.

I stayed at the doctor-vet home for the whole day. I spent time with My-Audrey and sometimes I had to be in the kennel by myself. I tried to tell them I know potty-potty, and it's okay not to put me in the go-to-work kennel. They didn't listen; Mom names this frustrating. For a while, I got to be in the room with all the Doctor Ladies. One of the nice girls came to love-touch me and I felt a sharp poke, hurt, and I got tired and went to sleep.

When I woke up, I was still tired and had a new hurt on my tummy and the not-good funny feeling inside my tummy. Mom came back to get me and take me home. She carried me up the stair-steps to the big fluffy bed. I was glad Mom carried me up the stair-steps because I am not sure I could have done it on my own. I don't know what happened, but my tummy had a big ouch on the outside, and it was loud hurt when I walked. I don't remember getting hurt so I don't know where it came from.

I was in the big fluffy bed with Mama and my tummy was itchy, so I licked and chewed on it. Mom used my No-No-No name, so I tried to stop because I don't like the No-No-No name. The tummy hurt was loud and very itchy so I licked it again. Mom told me she was sad I have don't-feel-good, and then she put something around my neck called a cone. The cone made it so I couldn't reach my tummy to lick it anymore. Mama said I look like her little flower.

I knew Mom worried because she kept touching and poking my tummy and saying, "It looks good." I love my mom very much, but I don't understand why she would let someone put the hurt on my tummy like that!

I didn't feel good on my tummy for a few days, so Mom gave me medicine wrapped in cheese. We didn't walk or have field play. After lots of days, she took me for a short-time walk, but I had to stay on the leash and couldn't run and play. After more days, I finally got to go for field and run! The hurt was gone! I was happy to run, but I still had a tugging in my tummy. Before long there was no more tugging in my tummy, things were back to normal! We went back to the doctor lady place; I got to smell My-Audrey, Patty, and the Doctor-Jackie. They told Mom I was healing.

I decided the doctor-vet home is where we go when Mom worries about us, or when something is not Ok-alright. Mom said "Doctor-People are for helping us feel better and fixing the hurt! Sometimes we have to hurt for a little while. This is another "best-for-you" I don't like. Sometimes Robbi and Joey go with Mom and I can smell they went to the doctor-vet home. One day Joey had the hurt and went away with Mom for a while. When he came back, I could smell that he went to the doctor-vet home.

~ Learning ~

I have figured out what lots of noises and words mean. I know when we are getting ready for a walk because I hear noises that mean Mom is getting collars and shoes. I can tell when we are getting treats because of the noise from getting them out of the treat place jar. I know right where to sit for a treat, and I know to be ready for Mom to find my mouth.

I know when people are coming to our home to smell us because I hear a knock or doorbell. Sometimes I'm wrong about knock and doorbell because the noise didn't come from by the door-hole; it came from Dad's be-quiet-I'm-watching-TV place. Mom helps me know when to listen for noises by saying things like "is Daddy home," or "who is here." I also know to listen for a knock or doorbell when Mom says Jeannie or Grandma and Grandpa are coming to visit.

Dad tells me words too, like "do you want to go," which means a car-truck ride. And "I'm going to bed," which means it is the long sleep time called night. Mom and Dad use lots of words I don't understand, but when I hear them a few times and the same thing happens, I can figure it out.

When Mom says, "I will vacuum," this means she will chase me around the home with the thing that makes a loud roaring noise in my ears. Robbi and I don't like the vacuum, Joey ignores it. When Mom or Dad says "I will pick up poop," this means they are walking around the yard outside and I can follow them if I want.

The thing Mom holds in her hand called phone makes many noises. Some of them mean nothing, but some of them I like. Sometimes the phone noise means we will see Martina. It makes different noises for seeing Danette and Sue too! I get very excited when I hear these noises. Sometimes Mom talks to the phone in her hand. If Mom needs to talk to the phone, she must be very lonely, so I try to help by crawling into her lap to say I am here and she can talk.

~ Happy Birthday One year ~

Well, it happened; I got the Happy Birthday "One Year" today! I hope this doesn't mean I won't have Happy Birthday "Months" anymore! I am excited to have another Happy Birthday because I get treats and toys and loves. But I'm sad because it means the end of my story. I have learned so much and smelled many wonderful people. Mom and Dad and Robbi and Joey are my family and my favorite people in the entire world! But I have so many who love and look out for me.

I know there is something special about me, but I'm not sure what the special is. Have I mentioned how cute and adorable I am? Mom also names me Happy and Inspiring. She says I have helped her with the carefuls in her life too. Mom's carefuls are different than mine but she said I have helped her in too many ways to count.

With help from all the people who love me, I figured out the stair-steps for the car-truck, I know not to follow Robbi and Joey when they chase noises, and I almost never run into carefuls at home now. Mom has lots of other new names for me too, like Perfect, Tenacious, Independent, and Determined! I haven't learned to cheat with the trick called seeing. But I have learned to use many other tricks, like listening and feeling.

We all have carefuls in our life and we need to rely on all our tricks to help us get where we want to go. When I first came to my new and forever home, it scared me and I was unsure it would be a good thing. I have learned so much and found so many wonderful things with my new family. What started as a scary thing for me has become the best thing in life, the love and happiness I have today!

There will always be carefuls in my life, but they don't have to stop me from the things that matter most. Carefuls are everywhere and I have learned I can find a different path to get to where I want to go!

My way may be different than yours, but I'm sure we want the same things. Happiness, Love and Security! Watch out for the carefuls in your life, but don't let them stop you from smelling new smells, feeling new feels, hearing new sounds, and loving more people.

I still have a lot to learn, and Mom is always teaching me new things. I'm looking forward to more adventures coming soon. If I am lucky, someday I will get to smell you! For now, know that you are special, cute, and adorable too! Love is my most bestest favorite thing ever, and everyone should feel loved for exactly who they are!

Don't let a careful in your way be the end of your story!

Keeper Malachi
Pederson

Keeper's Family

Note from the author (Keeper's Mom):

When I heard about Keeper, I knew I had to reach beyond my apprehensions and do everything I could to help this little girl find her best life. I have learned that in spite of her physical challenges, Keeper is driven, intuitive, open and accepting. I fell in love with Keeper the first time I met her sweet little face, and I knew she was a special girl. Keeper has given me so much. My love and respect for Keeper has pushed me beyond my comfort zone, made me reach for ways to share her story I never imagined myself capable of.

I made a conscious choice not to coddle or be over-protective of Keeper; to allow her every opportunity to embrace life, test boundaries, reach for adventures and enjoy every minute. She has not disappointed! Keeper is a happy, independent, resolute, little soul. She has made my life infinitely better with her sweet little face and unconditional love. I hope by sharing Keepers' story you can find a few smiles and the good feelings she seems to bring to everyone she meets. I don't know how long I will be blessed with Keepers presence; I do know that every minute is a gift beyond measure!

In my life for just a part, you are forever in my heart!

Thank you for reading my story, a portion of the proceeds from this book will be donated to the Morris Animal Foundation, Golden Retriever Lifetime Study!

Golden Retriever Lifetime Study: The Golden Retriever Lifetime Study is one of the largest, most comprehensive prospective canine health studies in the United States. The study's purpose is to identify the nutritional, environmental, lifestyle and genetic risk factors for cancer and other diseases in dogs. Each year, with the help of veterinarians and dog owners, the Foundation collects health, environmental and behavioral data on 3,000+ enrolled golden retrievers.

https://www.morrisanimalfoundation.org/golden-retriever-lifetime-study

Hero #2644 Joey Pederson

Made in the USA
Columbia, SC
10 January 2020